Attic Dolls

MILNER CRAFT SERIES

Attic Dolls

Linda Carroll

THE CREATION AND DESIGN
OF ARTIST'S DOLLS

SALLY MILNER PUBLISHING

Page 2: Attic Doll Dressed in Antique Lace

Antique lace is dipped into a soft 'mushroom pink' dye and then into blue. The lace is draped over 'old gold' satin. Subtle and unusual combinations of fabric and colour are arrived at through experimentation.

*Below: **Old Dolls House***

This doll house is from my private collection. It may be used in a purely decorative way. I frequently use it as a display element, in conjunction with dolls.

Page 6: Attic Dolls Dressed in Velvet and Brocade

The soft apricot velvet is trimmed with antique French Lace which has been dipped in ochre dye. This gives a gently aged appearance. The Swiss straw hat with cascading net sets off the 'old moss-green' and antique brocade worn by the accompanying doll. Green and pink details lend an 'old world' appearance.

Page 7: Attic Dolls Wearing Pink Velvet Ruched with Pearls

Old gold brushed over the ruching adds an aged patina which softens the whole effect. Beaded trims offer a limitless variety of romantic effects.

First published in 1994 by
Sally Milner Publishing Pty Ltd
558 Darling Street
Rozelle NSW 2039
Australia

©Linda Carroll, 1994

Design by Stan Lamond, Lamond Art & Design
Illustrations by Linda Carroll
Photographs by Peter Liddy
Printed by Singapore National Printers

National Library of Australia
Cataloguing-in-Publication data:
Carroll, Linda (Linda Elaine).
Attic dolls

ISBN 1 86351 128 8.

1. Dollmaking. 2. Doll clothes. I. Title. (Series: Milner craft series).

745.59221

CONTENTS

PREFACE

LINDA CARROLL'S mastery of the timeless art of doll-making is clearly apparent in each exquisite piece created in her studio. A highly accomplished artist, she studied painting at the Western Australian Institute of Technology in Perth and, in 1973, soon after graduation, joined her artist-husband, Michael Taylor in South Africa. There she established her studio, taught part-time at the University of Natal and began exhibiting her paintings in Durban and Cape Town.

While in Africa, Linda extended her painting skills to include objects she either made or found. Inspired by traditional African art, she began a lively series of exquisitely carved wooden and moulded clay figures, to which she refers as her 'leaf creatures' and 'clay people'. During her eight years in Africa, she travelled widely and was profoundly inspired by the great variety of cultures she experienced and by the richness of their art and craft forms. Her experiences in Africa and, more recently, her many trips to Bali continually enhance her love of elaborate decorative imagery, exotic and richly decorated and patterned surfaces, lush colour combinations and textures and the magical transformation of the common into the extraordinary. This, together with a disciplined design sense and active imagination, has meant that she excels at everything she puts her hand to. It was in Queensland that she developed yet another facet of her creative talent, the art of doll making.

Above & Opposite: Boxed Assemblage with Figures

An early artwork incorporating my first porcelain figures. The old cutlery box contains 'leaf creatures' sleeping amidst the seashells. The interior lid of the box is tin, decorated with repoussage.

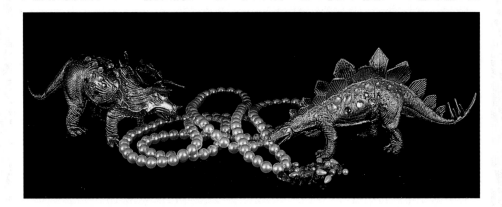

Jewelled Dinosaurs Eating Pearls
These plastic dinosaurs have been sprayed with antique gold and decorated with jewels. The transformation is typical of the effects that may be achieved from using beading on crowns etc.

Linda Carroll did not make a conscious decision to become the well-known doll-maker she has become, rather her interest and expertise in this age-old art form simply evolved. She developed a series of rag dolls from materials which were readily at hand. Their basic shape was much like gingerbread men; using her imagination and paint, lacquer, odd bits of material and bead work, she transformed this humble form into captivating little images akin to her sculpture. Delighted family and friends encouraged her to display these highly original rag dolls publicly. Much to her surprise, Linda had immediate success, with a number of serious collectors captivated by her work. Indeed, her large, highly appreciative audience has stimulated the continued evolution of her designs.

Linda Carroll collects and values things that have inherent imperfections, such as Turkish and tribal carpets, Indian and western embroidery, cracked and mended Mexican pottery, worn bits of lace, beadwork and cloth from second-hand and antique shops, and which possess qualities she believes links them with their makers and the people who have used them. Her dolls reflect these preferences; the mass-produced look is consciously avoided and they never resemble types of dolls that have been historically popular. Linda strives to produce little beings who are in a class of their own and with which people can immediately identify; they can confide in them and confer upon them a special personality. She approaches the making of each doll as if it is the only one she will ever make, believing this allows them their individual voice and personality. As in all of her creative work, she loves bringing an idea alive, giving it purpose and special significance for herself and her appreciative audience.

Linda's well known Attic Dolls are her most recent and have evolved from her charming rag doll series. More elaborate, with skilfully moulded porcelain heads, hands and feet and a much more complex body structure, they pay homage to earlier doll forms while retaining a timeless quality and, of course, Linda's individual touch.

Linda continues to use fabrics, embroidery and beadwork that have enjoyed a former life and which she gathered from second-hand and antique shops, or from clients who commission her to incorporate material from a favourite dress in the doll's fabrication. She deeply believes these materials possess a unique magic derived from their previous owners. She also likes the 'special feel' she gets from the basic ingredients used in her work - clay, paint, beads, old lace and cloth, and responds to their individual properties, transforming them into 'something special, something that people can identify with and treasure'.

Linda's Attic Dolls series allows her to explore all sorts of possibilities, like searching through an attic full of hidden treasures. It provides her vivid imagination total freedom to explore and utilise visual and tactile sensations and sources of inspiration as diverse as architecture, religious icons, and exotic birds and animals. She delights in the transformation of the mundane into something magical and 'otherworldly'. Her Attic Dolls receive equal attention and devotion to detail as her other creative pursuits. It is in this way that she fleshes out her own unique view of the world. This is more than mere escape, for this artist pursues the essential verification of her highly personal notion of existence through her work. Utilising attractive forms and materials, she has achieved what so many artists attempt but fail to do, that is, the creation of that essential bridge between the objective world and their personal visions. Her dolls, along with all she creates, provides immediate accessibility to her complex subjective imagery. This is what makes her work so appealing.

Linda Carroll hopes that this book will inspire others to explore and experiment with the wonderful art of doll-making. She wants those who are interested to pursue a personal direction, discovering in the process their own freedom to create something both original and meaningful. Readers are encouraged to use the basic forms and instructions contained on these pages as starting points for their own personal journey of discovery and self fulfilment. Doll-making can be a highly rewarding artform, which its long history so adequately demonstrates. Its magic and special appeal has never diminished because it directly addresses those innate qualities that makes us all part of the human family.

DAVID SEIBERT
Queensland College of Art, Griffith University, 1993

INTRODUCTION

~❧~

*M*y initiation into the world of dolls came about as a consequence of a lifelong fascination with the human form. I realised recently that, although unaware of the significance of my actions, I had spent over two decades collecting human figurines. I now seldom return from an overseas visit without acquiring a new modelled or carved figure. Many of my first dolls were collected whilst living in Africa; these included Masai fertility dolls, Yoruba Ibeji figures and ritual dolls from many other African tribal groups. Indonesian puppets and old Chinese dolls were unearthed in English antique markets. The Chinese dolls were usually in tatters, frequently with a shoe missing.

Throughout this early period, I spent many hours making small art objects and installations which usually housed little people. I carved and modelled small 'leaf people', angels and sleeping effigies, using wood and porcelain. The figures were intricately painted and placed into boxes made specially to house each piece. The boxes were also painted and embellished until they became an integral part of the artwork. I carved my dolls with basic tools such as a small penknife, simple gouges and lots of sandpaper. All of this activity captured my imagination and I became totally involved in making facsimiles of little spirited people, all living their own very private lives in the environments that I had made for them.

As I became increasingly familiar with the processes of making my little people I also became more familiar with 'mainstream' doll-making and discovered that the processes that I had used as a fine art student had direct application in the making of dolls. My art school studies in painting and drawing, in slip-casting for ceramics and in modelling, carving and casting for sculpture all assumed a new importance for me - as did my studies in textiles and dyeing techniques. I had become a doll-maker.

*Opposite: **Attic Doll in Gold Lace***
The Attic doll wears a dress dipped in gold and a lace coat trimmed with pearls.
Trails of old Swiss netting fall around her shoulders.

DESIGNING AND MAKING A DOLL

$\mathcal{D}$oll-making is a rewarding, but demanding, occupation. It combines a number of different crafts and techniques, many of them very time-consuming. I have found that a doll-maker must be a sculptor, painter, carpenter, carver, potter, dressmaker, milliner, hairdresser and make-up artist. Above all, the doll-maker must be patient. She, or he, must be prepared to spend heroic amounts of time in the studio. For without commitment and a preparedness to 'put in the hours', very little of worth is likely to be achieved.

I don't consciously 'design' my dolls. However, I generally have a pretty good idea of the style and feeling for which I am aiming. I make no preliminary drawings and rely very much upon a broad concept. This concept is progressively refined during the production process. I rely very much upon intuition and upon a sound knowledge of my resource material.

For the style of dolls that I make it is very important to have access to a wide range of appropriate resource material. In my case, this includes historical and contemporary books on art, fashion, decor, botany and textiles. Also, I find that I am inspired by films and documentaries that I have seen and by my own travels. I am very drawn to the romantic and have a passion for fantasy and decoration. Maybe this is why I am so fond of opera and Balinese music and why they both form a constant accompaniment to my working day.

In the following pages I outline how I make my dolls and make a number of suggestions regarding materials and techniques. I hope that this will provide you with both the inspiration and the basic knowledge to make your own original doll creations.

Opposite: Doll in Dove Grey

Dove grey French lace embossed with a multitude of silvery-grey seed pearls. The dress is trimmed with pink tassel braid. Swiss straw hat with pale grey and pink flowers.

INTRODUCTION TO MOULD-MAKING

If you decide to sculpt a little doll, you will find that there is a wide range of materials from which to choose. Dolls may be made with synthetic materials such as Cernit, Sculpy or Fimo and home-made materials such as papier maché are also useful. All are readily available and are ideally suited to the doll-sculptor who wishes to make 'one of a kind' dolls. It is simply a matter of finding which material best suits your intentions.

The intimacy of working with these particular materials is very exciting and could absorb one to the exclusion of any other processes and materials. However, if you wish to produce a certain number of similar dolls, such as I did with my 'Attic Doll' series, you will have to consider the use of slip-cast moulds. You will note that I say 'similar' and not 'identical'. Slip-casting is an extremely useful means of reproducing sculptural forms, but for the doll to be truly original, I believe that the subsequent treatment should make each doll similar, but unique.

THE MODEL

I suggest that you use plasticine, or some similar modelling material, to make the original piece. This material has the advantage of remaining malleable throughout the modelling and casting process and does not carry the risk of shrinking, drying and cracking that is associated with clay. Wax is also useful for the original sculptural piece but, as any child will tell you, plasticine is fun! It is also a very easy material with which to work.

Once you have played around a bit with the medium and have gained some confidence in modelling you should concentrate upon making features for your little doll with which you feel happy. It is very important to follow some simple proportional rules in modelling the head and face. Facial expressions may be indicated when you are at the painting stage, but it is necessary, at this stage, to establish a number of basic proportions. The head may be divided into three equal proportions: from the hair-line to the eyebrows; from the eyebrows to the tip of the nose; from the tip of the nose to the chin. The top of the ears are just below the level of the eyebrows. The eyes are halfway between the top of the head and the chin. These proportions may be faintly scribed into the modelling material as a guide. If you are also making the limbs, remember you should do so at this stage so that you can make the required number of moulds for your doll.

MAKING THE MOULD

When you have modelled the piece to your satisfaction, you should prepare to make the mould. If you follow the accompanying illustrated instructions you will learn to make a basic wooden form, or box, that may be changed to accommodate modelled pieces of many dimensions.

Having completed the moulding box which will contain your piece of sculpture, you should prepare the piece by making a line around the intended seam. This is very important, as the mould must divide into two separate pieces in order to extract the cast. The line must be lightly drawn, using a fine point around the widest part of the model. Care should be taken to avoid 'under-cuts', or pieces which might get caught when the mould is separated. In general, the seam line runs across the top of the head, down and along the line of the ears and straight down either side of the neck from the lobes of the ears. If your model includes a shoulder piece, the line will run from the base of the neck along the highest part of each shoulder. Needless to say, hands always present a particular problem for slip-casting. This accounts, to a large extent, for the relatively simple positions of most slip-cast hands. When modelling hands, it is best to do so with ease of casting in mind in order to balance expressiveness with practicality!

When the model is complete and the seam line established, you should then place the model in the moulding box and run a clay or plasticine roll lightly around the seam line. The box should then be filled with clay or plasticine up to the seam line. Your model will now be half embedded. At this stage you should also make sure that the joins in your box are filled with plasticine or clay, as you are now about to fill the box with liquid moulding plaster and it must not leak out through the joins.

To mix the plaster, use a flexible plastic bowl of a suitable size. The next part should be done very quickly, as plaster solidifies with frightening speed and you can easily end up with a bowl of solid plaster! You should part-fill the bowl

Attic Dolls

with water and then pour sufficient plaster of Paris into the bowl to make a creamy consistency when mixed with your hands. A 'rule of thumb' recipe for plaster mixing, taught to me at art school, was to part fill the container with water and then add plaster steadily until a small cone of plaster appeared above the liquid. Strangely, this has proven to be a reliable method! You should make sure that there are no lumps of undissolved plaster. Now pour the mixture into the box, right up to the brim, or deep enough to ensure that the model is covered by at least 40 mm ($1\frac{1}{2}$") of plaster. The following instruction may seem odd, but you should now strike the worktable repeatedly with your fist, or lift one end of the table very slightly and drop it a few times; this will ensure that any air bubbles rise to the surface instead of sticking to the model and causing problems later on.

Leave the mould to dry for an hour or so. You will notice that the plaster gets very hot while it solidifies. Once it has cooled, you can unlock the box, turn the mould over and remove the clay, or plasticine, in which the model is embedded. The model should remain in the plaster half-mould.

You may at this point, if you wish, make a couple of 'keys' on the face of the half-mould. This helps to line up the mould halves when you are preparing to pour the porcelain cast. The keys are simple to make with a small coin by turning it lightly a couple of times into the still-damp plaster in order to make two slight, smooth depressions.

Place the half-mould back into the box, seal the edges again and cover the face of the mould with a thin layer of vaseline or liquid soap, which acts as a 'release agent' to stop the two halves from sticking together. If this is not done correctly, it is probable that the two halves will be joined permanently. You should now mix the plaster and pour it over the exposed piece of the model to the same depth as the first 'pour'. When the second 'pour' is hardened, the box may be removed and the two halves separated. Often a gentle tap will be required around the seam line to open it for the first time.

When the two halves are separated, you should gently remove the model, as you may need to make several more moulds from the same piece. You now have a 'two-part mould'. You should finish the outside of the mould neatly with a plane or 'Surform' rasp. Now repeat the whole process until you have the required number of moulds (arms, legs, etc.) for your particular doll.

An important thing to remember is that you should never, never pour plaster down the sink when you are cleaning up! Collect all plaster residue and place it in the refuse bin. This is where the flexible bowl comes in handy; it only has to be flexed a bit to release all the dried plaster.

18

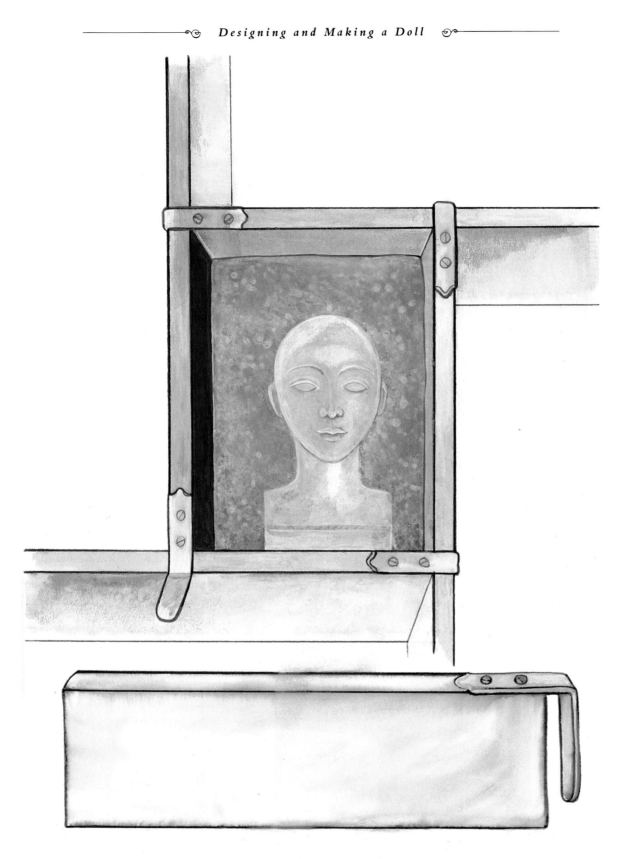

A simple casting frame

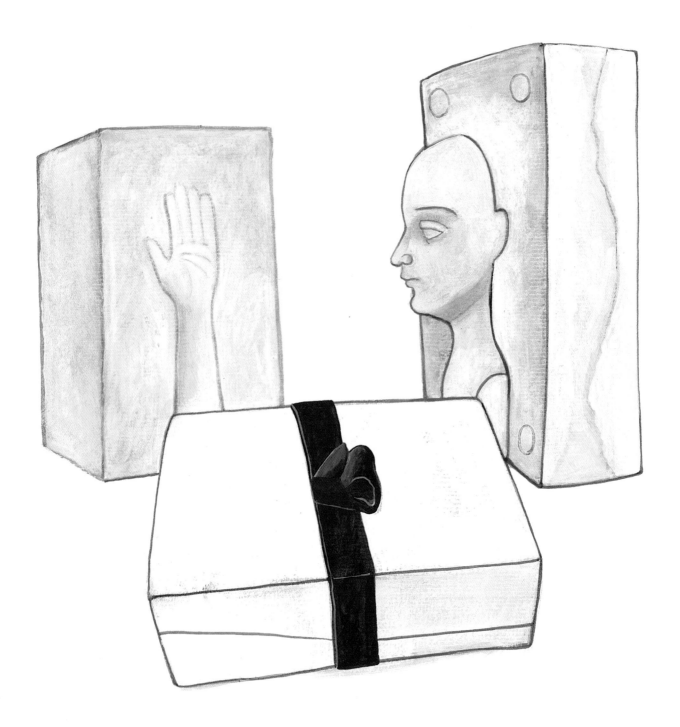

A finished plaster mould—
note the plaster 'kegs' and rubber-band fastening

The moulds should now dry for at least five days before being used. This is very important as, although they may feel dry to the touch, they will retain water for some days. Any attempt to use the moulds before they are truly hardened will result in the plaster disintegrating. You should also resist any impulse to speed up the drying process by placing the moulds in the oven, as this can break down the components in the plaster.

Once the moulds are really dry, they should be joined in readiness for casting. They should also be joined for storage when not in use; this helps to protect the delicate inner surface of the mould. I use rubber bands made from old inner tubes to secure the two halves.

Slip-Casting

I use porcelain slip for casting. This may be obtained ready-mixed from any reputable pottery supplies store. You may also mix your own, but I don't advise it as it is difficult and time-consuming to achieve the right consistency. You should make sure that the moulds are well-secured before pouring. Once the slip is poured you must gauge how long it should be left before being emptied. This will determine the thickness of the porcelain. I like a bit of weight to my dolls, so I tend to leave the slip in a little longer than would normally be recommended. It is all a matter of preference. You will notice the level of the porcelain slip dropping, leaving a higher ridge around the edge of the mould, this will give you some indication of the thickness that it has reached. The dry plaster is very porous and will quite quickly absorb moisture from the clay.

When the porcelain has reached the preferred thickness, you should pour the excess back into the porcelain container. If the piece that you have cast is quite small, you can possibly remove it from the mould in about 20 minutes; there are, however, a lot of variables. The size and thickness of the mould and the ambient humidity will all affect the time required. For instance, on a rainy day the time is greatly extended. Also a mould that has been recently used will absorb moisture much more slowly.

When the moulds have been split and all the pieces removed, they should be allowed to harden to a 'leather-hard' consistency. At this stage it is safe to handle them. You can now sit down and trim the seam along the edges using a thin blade such as a craft knife or penknife.

Once the seams have been cleaned, go over the cast with a damp brush or small sea sponge to remove any imperfections. It is also possible to allow the cleaned cast to dry out and finish the surface off with a very fine grade of steel wool. Should you decide to do the latter, do so out of doors and use a dust mask, as the dust can be very messy and is also an irritant. Use a '00' grade of steel wool, or finer. Anything coarser will mark the clay.

The cleaned parts should now be set aside to dry thoroughly before being placed in the kiln. This will take several days; even then there will be moisture within the clay which must be dispelled by gentle preheating once it has been placed in the kiln.

Moulds and Casts
*Cast porcelain figures ready for the kiln. A collection of
plaster moulds accompanied by an assembled doll.*

FIRING THE KILN

My kiln is my absolute pride and joy. I had always felt a bit inadequate when it came to technical equipment and thought that I would never be able to load and fire my own kiln. It all seemed very daunting, particularly when I listened to potter friends waxing technical! They all seemed to talk constantly about cones, firing times and bizarre explosions. It began to sound pretty dangerous.

Anyway, the big day arrived and I finally had my very own kiln. It was a very small electric kiln but could easily accommodate the parts for ten dolls at a time. The kiln was carefully installed in my studio and I regarded it with some trepidation. After reading the manual, though, I began to realise that the mysteries were a bit overplayed. The firing times and basic temperatures for earthenware and porcelain were clearly indicated, and I found that it was as easy as baking a cake. Easier actually, as I have never yet had a failed firing, nor a successful cake!

I always wait until I have enough pieces to fill the kiln before I have a firing. As I don't do any glaze firing, my kiln furniture is pretty minimal: one shelf and four supports. For the same reasons, I can stack the kiln pretty tightly.

My advice to beginners is 'Read the instructions'. The manufacturers know their product and the clay suppliers specify the preferred temperatures for their respective clays. I have found suppliers and manufacturers to be a good source of technical information if I require any help. There are also plenty of good, sensible books for beginner potters which apply equally to doll-makers.

MAKING THE BODY

There must be countless methods of body assembly and articulation. The simplest method would be to make a stuffed calico body, upper arms and legs. I have experimented with a variety of techniques, ranging from articulated wooden limbs to soft bodies and internal armatures. There are also a number of proprietary body articulation and armature systems available commercially. Suppliers of articulating armatures advertise frequently in the various doll-making journals.

A simple method, and one which I frequently use, involves a soft body and a flexible internal armature with porcelain head and limbs. I cut out a very simple body suit which conveys the basic proportions that I wish the doll to have. I prefer to use a commercially available quilted fabric for this, though calico or cotton would be fine. Having made up my simple body suit, I insert a wire armature which has been previously threaded through plastic tubing to protect the metal from corrosion and to give the armature more 'body'.

The nice thing about using armatures is that they act as an internal skeleton, thus enabling you to arrange the completed doll in an expressive and natural position. Once the armature has been inserted into the body suit, I insert polyester fibre into the arms, legs and body until they feel nice and firm. To do this, I press the fibre down with a wooden tool. I find a chopstick very useful, as it reaches right into the extremities.

Now the little body is really beginning to take shape. The next step is to attach the head and limbs. This may be done in a variety of ways. They may be either sewn firmly into place or attached with a good adhesive. Once this stage is complete, the fun really starts. You now have all the excitement of deciding how you will paint the features; this is the point at which the personality of the doll is determined.

PAINTING THE DOLL

My dolls differ from many contemporary dolls in that they are painted and lacquered, not glazed. The eyes are painted also as I do not use the commercially available glass or plastic eyes. This enables me to give each doll a very personal quality. Before applying colour, I prime the surface with Gesso. This is a commercially available plaster and size primer. Although I did not realise this when I first started, this is actually a very early technique.

I use a good, artist's quality, water-based acrylic paint for my dolls. I apply the paint with a range of sable brushes, from tiny '00' grade brushes to large flat wash brushes. Water colour may also be used for delicate, transparent washes. It is possible to use sabeline, or even the very much cheaper squirrel-hair brushes, but they don't keep their shape well and will probably, in the end, prove to be a false economy.

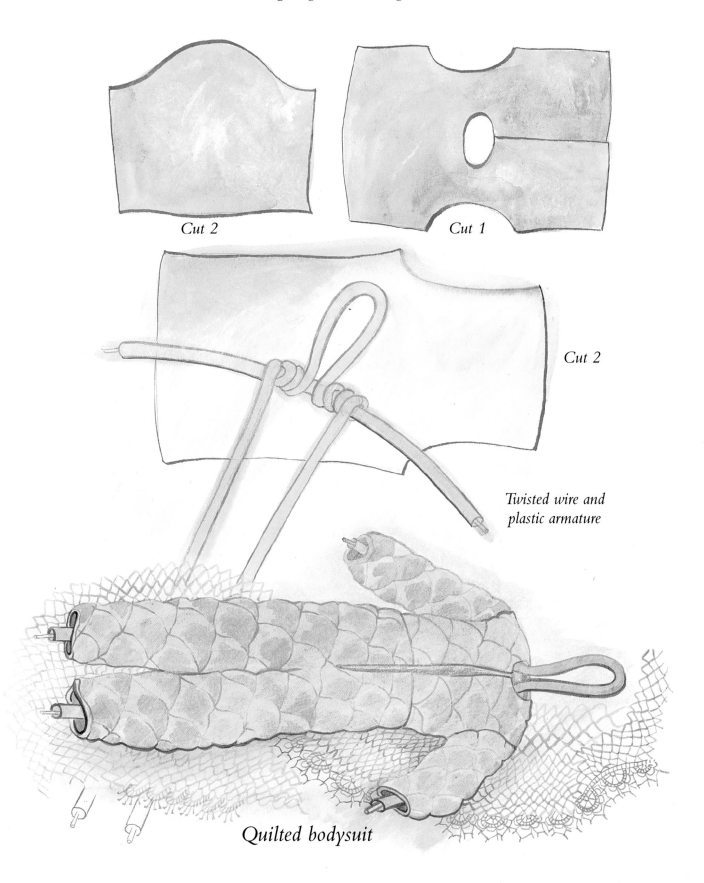

Cut 2

Cut 1

Cut 2

Twisted wire and plastic armature

Quilted bodysuit

There are a number of excellent proprietary lacquers on the market. The lacquers and varnishes may be purchased in high gloss, low gloss or matt finishes. It is a matter of preference which you use, but I prefer a clear gloss finish. I do not recommend water-based varnishes as these may, on occasion, cause problems by mixing with and dissolving your water-based paints.

Once you have your doll's body completely assembled, you are ready to start the creative process that will determine just what sort of little personality you are bringing into the world. Whether she, or he, is going to be a charming little Indian dressed in a brocade coat and bejewelled turban, a European child, a tragic heroine or a fantasy angel is entirely your decision.

On a practical level, the first step is to mix and apply a base coat, or overall skin colour to the little doll. It's a good idea to mix more colour than you might expect to use. In my experience the unexpected frequently occurs and an extra supply of the correct paint can be a blessing for touching up.

Naturally, the facial features are going to be the most important part of the painting. This part can be a disaster if you fail to follow some simple preliminary steps in order to establish, in particular, the levels and directions of the eyes. You will have already indicated the position of the eyes in your sculpted head but you should now draw a faint line across the head at this level, along which you will place the pupils. Next you should indicate the direction of the gaze by placing a dot on each eye, in the required position, taking care while doing so. There could be little worse than completing the whole face only to find that your little person has hideously crossed eyes! Much the same applies to the mouth; you should faintly draw in the line of the lips and ensure that this, also, is level. It is as well to spend some time over this task, as the eyes, eyebrows and mouth determine the expression.

Many amateur doll-makers buy ready-to-pour moulds, or even greenware that only requires firing. They are concerned with painting features that reproduce exactly a particular style of contemporary or historical doll. Their concern will extend to the precise number of eyelashes or the exact shape of the mouth in order to resemble most closely the doll that they are reproducing. This does not apply to us. We are concerned with creating our own little person. There may well be imperfections; perfect symmetry is rare in human faces and it is not unusual to have eyes of slightly differing sizes or a nose that is not precisely centred. It may be that our dolls will assume some of our own imperfections - this is one of the things that makes the whole process so exciting. As an art student, I was frequently intrigued by the fact that other students' life-drawings frequently bore more than a passing resemblance to themselves!

I sometimes look closely at dolls from another era, or culture, and I find that what endears them to me, reaches out and tugs at my imagination, is an internal 'presence'. A presence that lives independently of the doll's maker and which reaches out across time and distance. When you reach the stage of painting your doll, your main objective must be to use all of your skill to make a face that has meaning for you. You should place interpretation above realism.

A Variety of Painted Doll's Faces

One of the most important stages of doll-making is the creation of the facial expression.
It is important to place interpretation above realism, in this instance, so that the individuality
of the doll shines through. Here are facial details of four Attic dolls, illustrating how
each one has its own personality.

DESIGNING THE CLOTHES

༺৹৹৹༻

Designing and making clothes for your doll will often require research and, possibly, a few trips to a favourite antique market. If you already have a good collection of fabrics from which to choose, it simply becomes a matter of picking the best, and most appropriate, combinations of colour and texture. I have a sufficient supply of fabrics in my studio to last several lifetimes, yet I find that nothing is quite so inspiring as an exciting new purchase, followed by a search for braids, trim and accoutrements to enhance the fabric. I will hoard fabrics, braids or even pieces of costume jewellery for years until the right combination comes together.

On the following pages I have provided a few patterns that may be adapted to almost anything that I need to design for my dolls. The dress pattern can be changed with a few minor alterations, such as adding length to the sleeves, adding a cuff, or gathering the hemline of the skirt. The same pattern, turned back-to-front, becomes a guideline for an angel's lace coat, or a brocade coat for an Indian boy. The mood, style or historical content that you seek to achieve may be enhanced by altering the hemline, by sewing combinations of beads and pearls and by responding to the intrinsic qualities of the particular fabric. I often think of my dolls as three-dimensional collages for which no restrictions apply. For instance, I am quite happy to make an Indian doll and then add a few gold sequined stars to her coat and a pair of golden wings. I frequently combine unexpected and unlikely materials. There is an element of play in this; setting one item off against another can give rise to new ideas and open up quite unexpected possibilities.

Opposite: *Attic Doll with Beaded Cloche Cap*
The doll wears a beaded cloche cap. The combination of deep maroon satin and of red and gold brocade lends a rich, sensuous quality. This quality is softened and aged through the use of old Swiss netting.

You can add and subtract until you arrive at the sort of balance that you need. Balance will be achieved also by your choice of colour. Violet, carmine, carmine rose, terre verte, and, of course, the ochres are among my favourites. Velvets, silk or lace dyed the same colour will give an interesting effect because you are then playing around with the same colour but with differing textures: soft and dull velvet; smooth, shiny, light-reflecting satin; delicate, intricate strands of lace. Play them off against each other, add the richness of gold braids or tasselled braids dyed in contrasting colours. By playing with texture and colour, you can give full rein to your imagination.

One of the really important things to remember is to use fabrics that are appropriate for the dolls you are making. If I am asked to make a little Indian boy, for instance, I will use the indigenous fabric, the 'genuine article'. I have a large collection of fabrics from many parts of the world, much of it acquired while on trips to Europe or Asia. I am in love with old fabrics; when travelling overseas I have a passion for inspecting, at close range, various fabrics in galleries, museum collections, market stalls and historic buildings. This holds a real fascination for me and is one of the reasons why I love making dolls. Many of my own fabrics have been given to me by people who have themselves hoarded them for years. Often they hold special memories from bygone days. Occasionally people will ask if I will make a doll for them from a special fabric, such as their own wedding dress. The choice of fabric is really important. If you use fabrics that you love and which evoke particular memories or emotions, you will make a doll that has a very special meaning for you, and for whoever else looks at it.

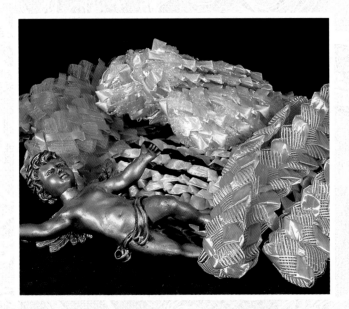

A Box of Swiss Straws
Swiss millinery straws may be dyed to lend an aged appearance and to blend in more effectively with the chosen ensemble.

Opposite:
Doll in Burgundy Lace
The doll wears burgundy lace embroidered with glass seed beads and antiqued gold braids. Painted deep green net stockings provide a daring contrast. The hat is decorated with old millinery flowers.

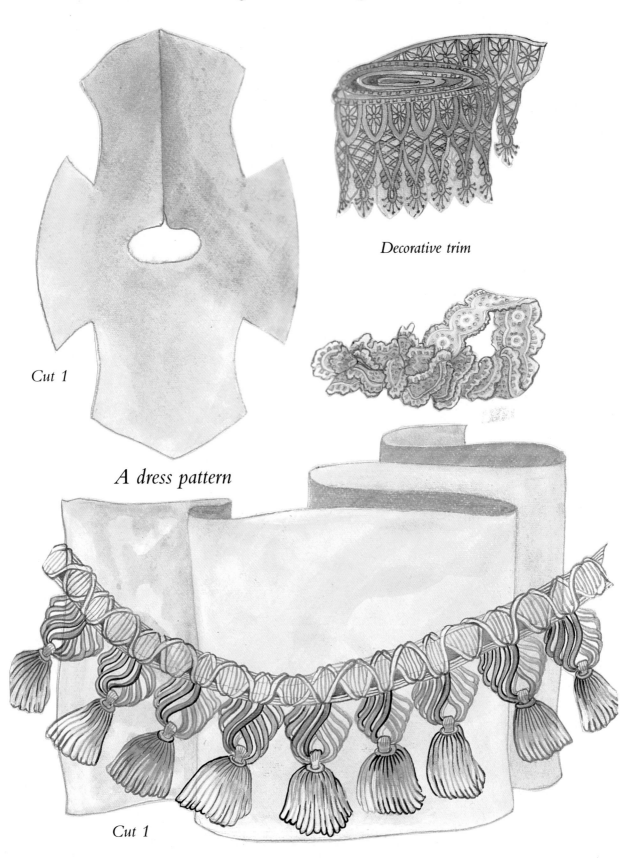

Cut 1

A dress pattern

Decorative trim

Cut 1

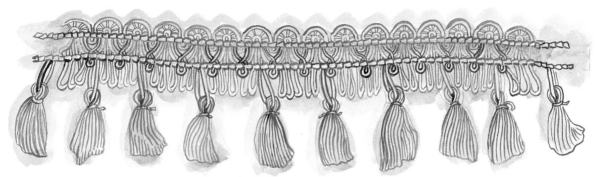

A petticoat pattern

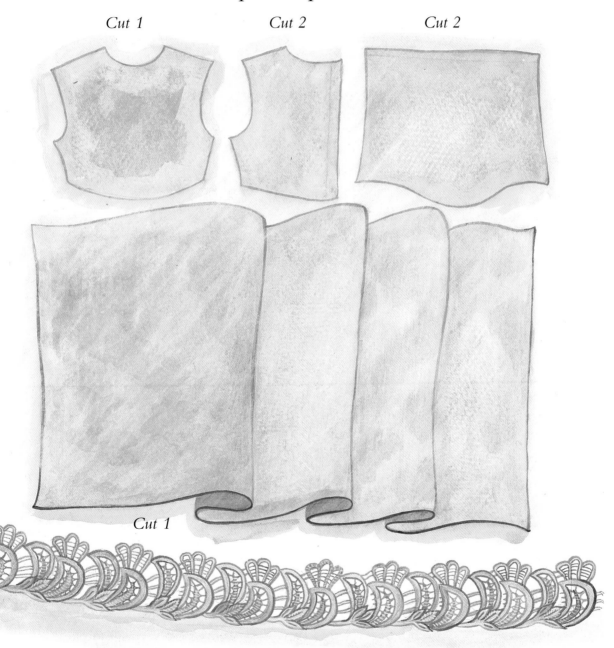

Cut 1   Cut 2   Cut 2

Cut 1

Braids and beading

Opposite: Doll in Old Ochre

The doll wears a variety of heavy lace, dyed in old ochre and trimmed with net and multitudes of pearls. The hat is dipped in the same dye batch. This colour lends a wonderful aged effect.

Angel's lace coat

Opposite: *Golden Angel*
The angel wears a gown which has been dipped into gold and given an antiqued finish.
The gown is trimmed with pearls.

Brocade coat for an Indian boy

Opposite: Kalish, the Indian Boy

The boy wears a rich burgundy knee-length coat over striped silk pantaloons.
Mirrored Indian embroidery is used on the bodice. The combination of authentic fabrics
gives an overall feeling of vitality.

Dolls in Lace

These small Attic dolls dressed in a variety of laces, serve as an example of the subtle colour changes that may be obtained by using different fabrics with the identical dye. The various textures and base colours of the fabrics will impart a surprising range of different colours.

Opposite: **Doll in Velvet Coat**

The doll wears a dusty-pink lace dress under a navy blue velvet, knee-length coat.
The coat is trimmed with antique pink rosettes.

DESIGNING AND MAKING HATS

In designing an ensemble for your doll it is important to take into account all sorts of cultural and historical considerations. I have experimented with many different ideas for hats and head-dresses. In general, I seek something that will give the doll a distinctive feeling and which will accentuate the particular characteristics of each doll. I have included a few very simple patterns in my illustrations. I find that by starting off with these basic designs I can then embellish them to my heart's content and will eventually come up with the sort of effect for which I'm looking. I am a firm believer in the power of decoration and elaboration. When things seem to go wrong, I seldom turn back; instead, I forge ahead. I find that, nine times out of ten, I will reach a happy solution if I keep going.

I take a lot of trouble with the design and making of hats. I am of the opinion that, from the creative viewpoint, it is not particularly rewarding simply to sew on bands and laces by machine. It is possible to do the really basic work with a machine, but the use of hand stitching for the application of braids, pearls and sequins is essential. So many little touches may be added; in particular, I am fond of small artificial flowers and feathers. The feathers may be found in millinery shops, pet shops or even while out walking. I've noticed that ballet shops and theatrical costumiers frequently display lovely varieties of feathers and small appliqué pieces which incorporate sequins, feathers and other decorative materials. Sometimes these may be used in their entirety or may be taken apart and used in another context.

I usually construct my hats upon one of two basic designs: the gored hat and the brimmed hat. Most styles of hat may be developed from these two designs. The gored hat fits the head closely and is suited to the construction of turbans, cloches, caps and helmets. The brimmed hat is self-explanatory and has a wide range of stylistic possibilities.

Opposite: **Doll in Silk Baby Coat**
The doll wears a crocheted silk baby coat over black and gold lace.
The hat is Swiss straw with an abundance of pink flowers and pale grey netting. A bunch
of old pink velvet flowers hangs from her waist.

A GORED HAT

Let us, for example, think of making a hat for an angel. The particular materials chosen, and the way in which they are put together will say everything. So, perhaps we will start with a five-gored hat, sewn from gold brocade. This could then be draped with Swiss net, or tulle, to give a soft, ethereal effect. The net could then be sewn into place with some decorative pearl braid. Another option would be to construct a little crown, or coronet, from black Fimo. This may have glass gems and pearls pressed into the crown until the surface becomes suitably rich and elaborate. Once the Fimo has been hardened in the oven, it can be painted gold, or even gilded with gold leaf. The coronet may then be placed around the gored hat and fixed into place with a little craft glue. The hat can be further embellished through the addition of silk flowers, perhaps sewn on with pearls. This will add further richness. Just keep on adding until you feel satisfied with the overall effect.

When I am making one of my little Indian boys or girls I like to make a five-gored hat from a rich brocade that will work well with the existing ensemble but which will, at the same time, add a bit of 'dash' or contrast. Velvet can also be very effective if you wish to play off a range of textures. Sew exotic scarves to bind around the hat in a turban style. Try to confine yourself to fabrics which have some cultural authenticity. A striped fabric and one in a rather exaggerated floral pattern, or a contrasting paisley, would look pretty exotic. Don't finish here, though! Try incorporating a variety of coloured beads of different sizes when sewing the scarves into position.

To really 'put the cherry on the cake', you might find authentic Indian jewellery to embellish the head-dress. I love seeking out these little goodies and am a regular visitor to flea markets and ethnic jewellery stalls. Were it not for the excuse of using such exotic paraphernalia for my dolls, I would never really have the opportunity of rummaging through mounds of trinkets and trimmings when travelling. When I make visits to Indonesia I spend many happy hours inspecting the beautiful gilt ornaments used in traditional dancing. In Europe, the antique markets have proved to be a valuable source of dress brocades, diamanté necklaces and costume jewellery from the fifties. Friends and relatives are also an invaluable source of doll material and very few return from trips without some wonderful fabrics or trinkets that they have picked up in street markets for me. Many of these pieces may be snipped apart with a pair of pliers and reassembled in a multitude of ways.

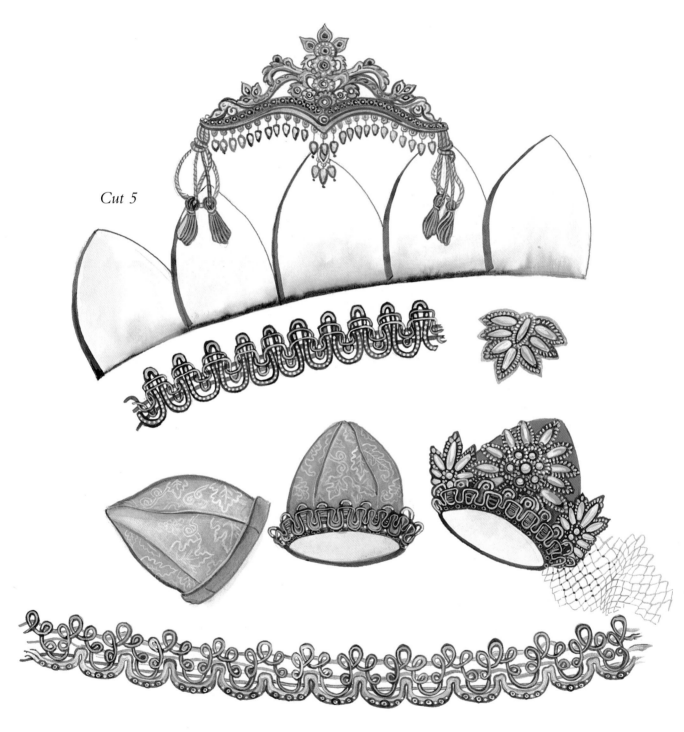

Cut 5

Pattern for a 5-gore hat

*Turban for an
Indian boy*

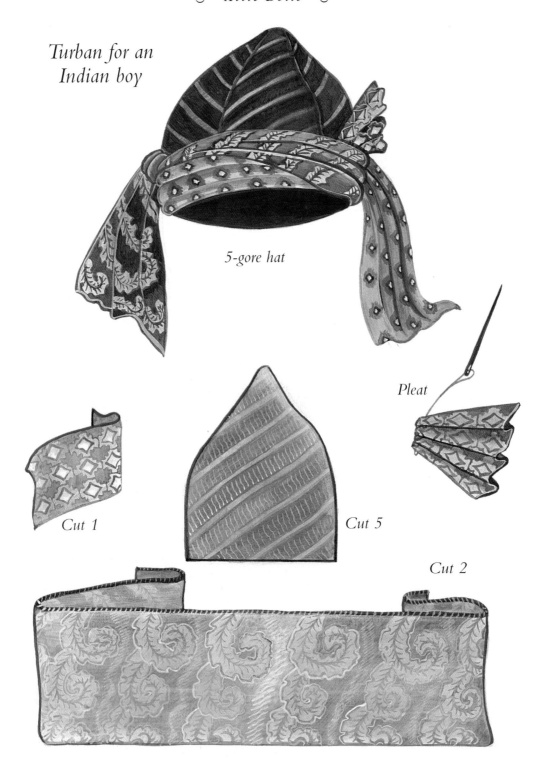

5-gore hat

Pleat

Cut 1

Cut 5

Cut 2

Opposite: Two Little Indian Children

*The two dolls wear authentic fabrics and are trimmed with richly coloured peasant jewellery.
The boy wears a deep-red velvet coat with green and yellow ochre braids. The girl wears a
heavy yellow ochre velvet dress trimmed with black and gold Indian braids.*

Two Little Indian Girls

The girls wear full dresses made from rich brocades and silk saris.
Contrasting colours are used to decorate the turbans. Brightly coloured
Indian jewellery accentuates the effect.

Opposite: Doll in Emerald Green

A rich emerald green watered taffeta contrasts with green, purple and
gold brocade from India. The ensemble is liberally trimmed with antiqued
gold braid and pearls.

A BRIMMED HAT

When designing a hat to complete the ensemble for, say, a little French or English doll, you will frequently need to design a style which has a wide brim - something that will encircle and frame the face with a variety of decorative elements. I love using French or Swiss straw for this. If you find it difficult to obtain the original straw in skeins, you can frequently find suitable original hats in antique markets or second-hand stores. These may be taken apart and used to make many little dolls' hats. I've spent many hours finding such hats and, all too frequently, I haven't had the heart to take them apart. The survivors now occupy prominent places in what I refer to as my 'inspirational collection'! Anyway, for those who are unable to find the original article, I have devised a pattern which is easily adapted for use on any doll for which a wide-brimmed hat is required. I have illustrated the various stages in the accompanying diagram.

This hat may be made from any material that you have at hand. Silk or velvet would probably prove to be the most suitable.

First cut out the pattern and lay it onto a stiff lining. Cut the lining. This will form the foundation, which must then be covered: the brim must be covered on both sides - I frequently use contrasting fabrics, textures or colours for this. The band and the crown are covered on one side only. Once they have been covered, you should take the band and sew it onto the brim, bringing the crescent-shaped perforations together.

When the band is joined to the rim, take the crown piece and sew it to the band, placing the round perforation at the back of the hat. You have now established the basic shape of the hat.

Any suitable trimmings may be used to decorate the hat, keeping in mind at all times the overall effect that you wish to convey. If you have used a particular antique lace or ribbon on the dress, it might be effective to use a little of the same material for rosettes or bows as hat trimmings. I usually try a variety of trims and pin them to the hat temporarily until I am satisfied that the right balance has been achieved.

Opposite: Doll in Dove Grey
Dove grey French lace embossed with a multitude of silvery-grey seed pearls. Navy blue straw hat trimmed with sap-green flowers and emerald-green netting.

You might strew artificial flowers around the brim, or pin posies in a variety of positions until you feel that you have achieved a good combination. The elements may then be sewn into position, incorporating, perhaps, a variety of beads and pearls. You might try adding French or Swiss net. Even the tulle, or net, used for ballet dresses can look very effective.

When I am designing and making up a hat, I usually dye most of the elements that I intend putting together. The commercial dyes that are obtained from pharmacies may be intermixed. It is therefore possible to achieve the precise colour or shade that is required. You will find that by dyeing the materials, you can create a more distinctive and unified appearance. Fabrics, whether they are Swiss straw, velvet, lace or silk flowers, will all take on a mellow and gently aged appearance, giving a lovely patina to the finished article. It is a purely personal aesthetic choice, but I find such treatments indispensible.

Opposite: Dolls in Organza and Lace

The doll on the left wears contrasting sap green organza trimmed with soft emerald and upholstery braid. The doll on the right wears antique pink and gold lace brocade.

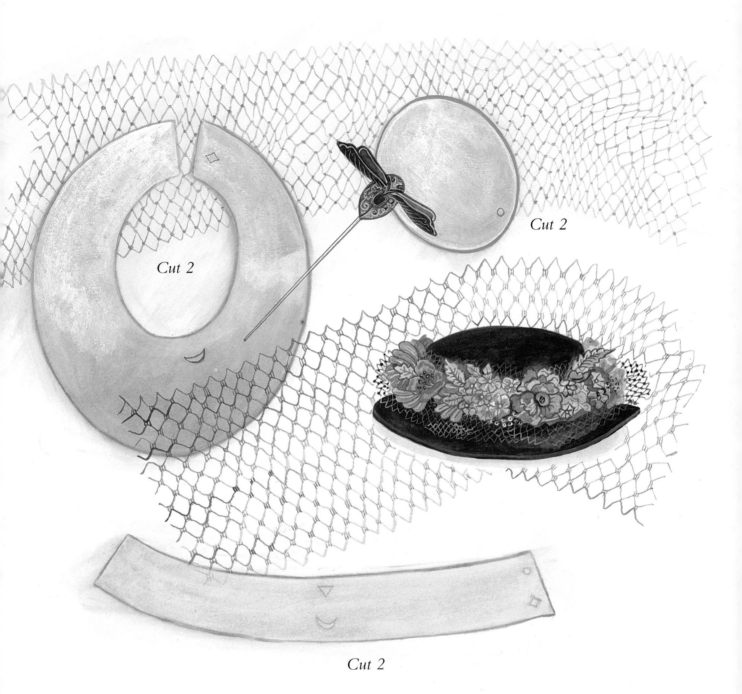

Cut 2

Cut 2

Cut 2

Pattern for a wide-brimmed hat

WINGS

When I first visited Bali I was amazed by the number of winged carved figures hanging from every ceiling. It was only later that I learnt that in Balinese mythology, the sky is the home of good spirits. This, of course, is common to many cultures. I am also captivated by the representations of angels in medieval, byzantine and renaissance paintings.

I use wings very frequently; some of my first little rag dolls were angels. The very first winged figures I made actually had feathered wings. These were carved sculptural figures and preceded the dolls by many years. I have since explored several ways of making wings and have found quilting to offer the best combination of softness and rigidity.

There is a very simple and effective pattern that I use frequently. It involves gold fabric filled with polyester fibre. First, you should lay your gold fabric, folded into four, on the cutting table. Place the wing pattern onto the fabric and cut, leaving a reasonable seam allowance. Sew around the wings, leaving the wide end open. This will enable the wings to be turned inside-out. I find that the ubiquitous chopstick is very useful for this job.

The wings should then be filled evenly, and moderately firmly, with polyester fibre. When you have done this, sew the end of the wing to enclose the filling. You should now quilt the wings into ribbed sections which will imitate the feather structure, whilst lending rigidity to the wing. You will have to decide whether to carry this out by hand or with the machine. Both methods will lend a strong sculptural effect.

When the wings have been quilted, they may be either left in this simple form or, alternatively, you might consider a few decorative treatments.

*Opposite: **Angel with Sequined Net***
Angel doll with 1920s black and gold sequined net overlay,
trimmed with bugle beads and pearls.

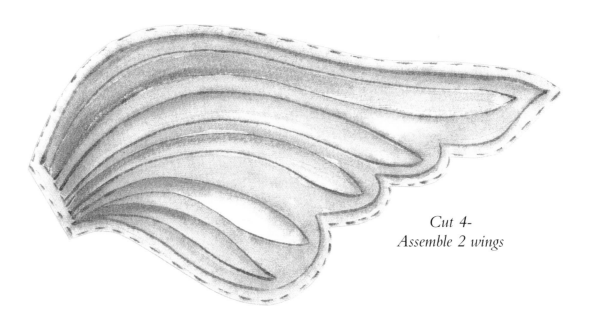

Cut 4-
Assemble 2 wings

Quilted wings for an angel

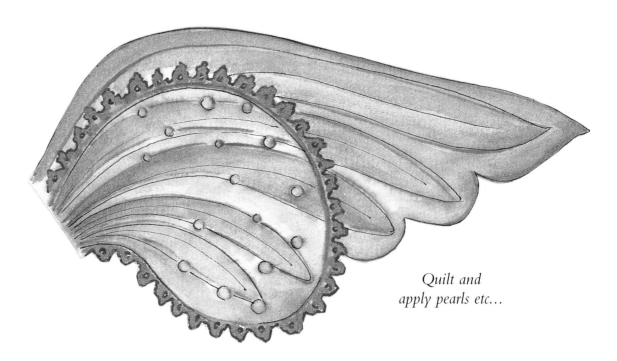

Quilt and
apply pearls etc…

Opposite: *Two Attic Dolls*

One doll wears an extremely old 19th century lace with metallic thread woven into
the fabric. This produces a gossamer, or spider web, effect. The other doll wears a lace dress
dyed in faded ochre overlaid with tulle embossed with pearls and antique lace.

SHOES

Many doll-makers are not prepared to undertake the fiddly and repetitive task of making shoes. Ready-made shoes may be purchased at most doll-makers supply shops. An excellent source of shoes and, indeed, most doll accessories, are the many doll fairs and exhibitions held throughout the year in most cities.

I seldom make use of ready-made shoes. Most of my dolls have shoes already modelled on their feet prior to firing. I find this to be the best solution and one that allows me to make far more stylish shoes. In particular, I am able to make high-heeled button-boots. This is a very traditional way of handling shoes and is a method you will find used on many antique dolls. I make removable shoes with some reluctance, and only on the rare occasions when they are absolutely necessary.

Modelling a shoe in clay

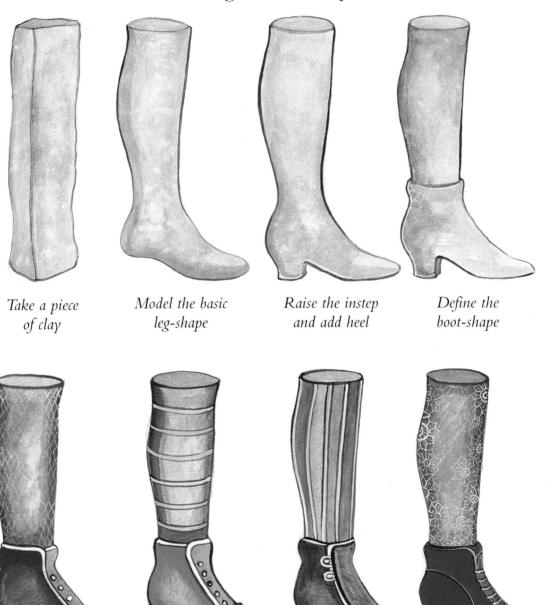

| *Take a piece of clay* | *Model the basic leg-shape* | *Raise the instep and add heel* | *Define the boot-shape* |

Make a plaster mould and cast legs as required. After firing, the stockings and boots may be painted in a variety of ways before varnishing.

Opposite: Doll in Emerald Green Dress

Emerald green and gold lace dress, trimmed with large diamante dress brooch and cascading violet Swiss netting. The hat is trimmed with gold braid and velvet leaves.

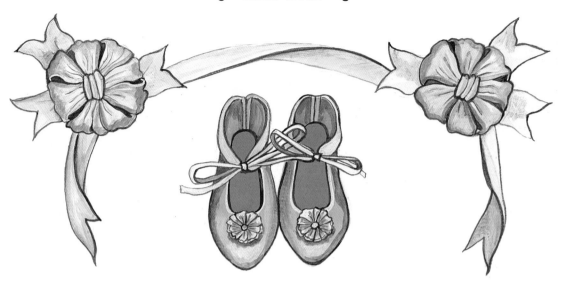

Shoes made from soft leather

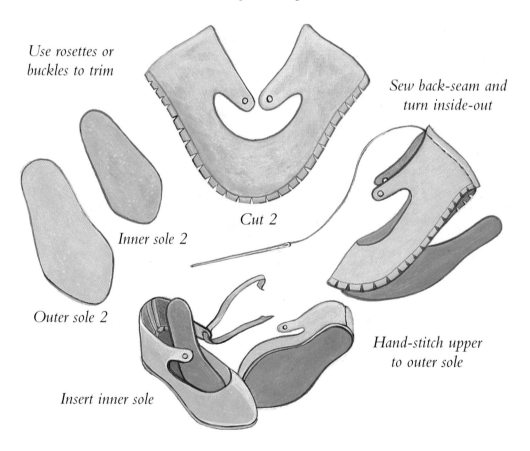

Use rosettes or
buckles to trim

Sew back-seam and
turn inside-out

Inner sole 2

Cut 2

Outer sole 2

Hand-stitch upper
to outer sole

Insert inner sole

Opposite: Princess Natasha

*Princess Natasha holds her own old Chinese doll. The dress is 'fin de siècle'
deep red satin, embroidered with tarnished metal thread. A coffee-coloured heavy
brocade lace coat completes the ensemble.*

DOLL COLLECTING

Doll collecting has, for many years, been a popular and absorbing pastime. It is also a very lucrative one. There is a ready market for rare or antique dolls and they are regarded by many as sound investments. Certainly the appreciation rate for rare dolls is astronomical.

There are many excellent journals devoted to dolls and collecting. Some are concerned primarily with identification and the historical aspects of doll collecting. Others are concerned with contemporary doll production.

Because of my occupation, I have been invited to view many collections. Some of them have been very orthodox and represent sound buying based upon knowledge and a nose for a good investment. Others have been idiosyncratic in the extreme, delightful and sometimes crazy collections of the wonderful and the bizarre. My own collection falls into the latter category. I have some very old dolls but I have never sought an appraisal of them. Their value is of little importance to me, but they are beautiful and I bought them because I loved them on sight. If I have any advice for prospective collectors it is 'trust your own judgement'. You may not end up with a priceless collection, but you will be surrounded by little personalities that you love and which hold precious associations for you. Whenever I look at my little people, I am transported back to wonderful moments of discovery in unlikely places. They have been my companions now for many years, and the family grows steadily as new arrivals swell their ranks. Friends bring little antique dolls back from overseas holidays and I find dolls in a wide range of expected (and unexpected) locations, including 'op shops', church fêtes and street markets.

Opposite: Attic Doll in Pink and Cream Brocade
The doll wears pink and cream upholstery brocade, trimmed with whimsical pom-poms. Swiss netting is draped around the well-worn straw hat. Silk fringing dipped in 'old gold' dye is worn around the shoulders.

This little book was written to introduce the reader to the intricacies and pleasures of doll making. For those readers who wish to make dolls, I hope that in following my simple explanations, you will find the inspiration for further experimentation and that you will be able to develop your own individual style. For those readers who simply have a love of dolls, I hope that you will gain as much pleasure from reading about my dolls as I have derived from making them.

Dolls in Straw Hats

The doll on the left is dressed in ruched navy blue French velvet trimmed with antiqued gold braid. The ensemble is coordinated with a hat of dyed Swiss straw trimmed with violets and red roses. The other doll wears deep red and gold brocade trimmed with pearls and gold braid. Her hat is antique gold Swiss straw trimmed with magenta flowers and old net.